When Workers Bleed
Thuli Marutle Leigh

ISBN: 978-1-997482-32-1
Cover Design: Thuli Marutle Leigh
Author: Thuli Marutle Leigh

DISCLAIMER

This book is inspired by real experiences, but names, workplaces, timelines, and identifying details have been changed to protect the privacy of all individuals involved. Any resemblance to actual persons or institutions is coincidental.

The purpose of this book is not to accuse, shame, or target anyone. It is a personal narrative exploring the emotional, physical, and professional challenges employees can face, and the impact workplace practices can have on human wellbeing.

This story is shared for awareness, understanding, and healing — not for legal judgment.

Dedication

To everyone who has ever worked while bleeding inside —
the ones who showed up even when their hearts, bodies, or minds were breaking.
This book is for the women, the men, and every worker who carried silent pain
because the world expected strength instead of humanity.
May you always remember that you are human first, and deserving of care.

✦ PREFACE

This is not only my story.
It is the story of workers everywhere — especially foreign teachers — who give more than their bodies can carry, more than their hearts can hold, and still show up because they care.

For a long time, I worked through exhaustion, untreated illness, emotional strain, and loneliness. I survived without a safety net, without insurance, and without the basic protections every worker deserves.

Then came the loss that changed everything — a grief I was not prepared for, and a workplace that viewed my pain as an inconvenience.

This book is not written out of anger, but out of truth.
Out of the need for compassion in workplaces.
Out of the belief that workers are human beings long before they are employees.

If this book makes even one employer choose humanity...
If it helps one worker feel seen...
Then it has done what it was meant to do.

✦ TABLE OF CONTENTS

PART I — BEFORE EVERYTHING FELL APART

CHAPTER 1 — THE JOURNEY BEGINS

When I first left home, I wasn't just boarding a plane — I was stepping into a new world. A world where nothing felt familiar, where every street, every sound, and every face reminded me that I was far from everything I once knew.

I didn't know that stepping onto that plane would change everything — not just my address, but my body, my spirit, and the way I understood work, dignity, and survival.

I left home with hope folded carefully into my luggage.
Hope for better opportunities.
Hope for stability.
Hope for a life where my hard work would finally mean something.

What I didn't carry — because no one warned me — was the emotional weight of beginning again in a place where nothing felt familiar. The streets, the people, the language, even the silence sounded different. I arrived with a brave face, but inside, I was a woman learning how to breathe all over again.

Every foreign worker knows this stage — the in-between.
Between excitement and fear.
Between new beginnings and quiet breakdowns.
Between telling yourself "I can do this" and whispering "I miss home."

I tried to convince myself that loneliness was normal.
That eating alone, sleeping alone, and crying quietly at night were just part of the journey.
That missing my husband and children until my chest tightened was simply something I had to endure.

I woke up every morning with one mission: to survive, to adapt, to be strong — even when no one knew how hard the nights really were.

But survival was not only about work.
It was also about learning how to exist in a place where very few people spoke English.
Where even the simplest tasks — buying food, finding a bus, asking for help — became daily tests of courage. Silence followed me everywhere, not the peaceful kind, but the kind that traps your words inside your throat because you know no one around you will understand them.

And then came an experience I never expected to face:
standing out everywhere I went.

As a woman of color in a city where almost everyone looked different from me, I carried a spotlight I never asked for. People stared. Some whispered. Many pulled out their phones to take pictures or videos, often without asking. Not because they were cruel — but because, for many, I was the first Black woman they had ever seen.

At first, I joked about it. I called them my paparazzi.
But the truth is — it wasn't always easy.

Being photographed while eating...
while shopping...
while simply walking down the street...
It was attention I never requested, and attention I didn't always know how to escape.

Then there were the curious touches — hands reaching toward my braids or natural hair with fascination, not disrespect. I could see the innocence in their eyes. But innocence doesn't erase discomfort. A simple, "May I?" would have turned those moments from invasive to human.

Living in a new country taught me something important:

People do not always realize they are hurting you

—

simply because they have never lived inside your skin.

I did not hate them for it.
I learned from it.
And I hoped they could learn from me too.

Because this chapter wasn't only about adjusting to a new place.
It was about adjusting to being seen in a way I never asked to be seen...
while still trying to build a life, make a home, and stay strong.

People think the journey begins when you start the job.
But for many of us, it begins long before that —
with sacrifices no one sees,
with fear hidden behind smiles,
and with courage we rarely get credit for.

I walked into this new life believing I would build something steady.
I didn't know that the place I was running toward would one day be the place that nearly broke me.

But this is where my story begins —
not with tragedy,
not with betrayal,
but with hope.

The kind of hope that makes people cross oceans, leave families behind, and rebuild themselves in places where even their name sounds foreign.

This was the beginning.
Before everything I carried became too heavy.
Before my body begged for rest.
Before the moment that changed everything.

This was the beginning of becoming stronger than I ever planned to be.

Chapter 2: Working Without a Pause

Work started before my body, mind, or heart had even adjusted to the new world around me. While everyone saw a teacher who showed up on time, smiling and prepared, they never knew the storm happening behind that smile.

The first three months were the hardest.

Because of the time difference between my country and the city I had moved to, my nights were never real nights, and my days were never real days. When it was daytime back home, it was the middle of the night for me — and my phone would buzz with messages, calls, updates from my husband and children. I couldn't ignore them. I was a mother first. A wife first. So I stayed awake, answering every call I could, because hearing their voices was the only thing keeping me from collapsing.

And when they didn't answer — when they were busy or asleep or out of reach — I would cry silently in the shower, the only place where no one could hear me break.

By the time morning came, I would have slept only two or three hours, sometimes none at all. But I still woke up on time for work every single day.

No one knew that I would call my family every morning their time — which was night for me — and every night their time — which was morning here. I lived in a constant loop of stretching myself between two worlds, never fully belonging to either one.

Sometimes, after hanging up, I would sit on the edge of my bed and feel the emptiness so strongly it felt physical.
It was the first time I had ever been away from my husband and children.
And the distance was heavier than all my suitcases combined.

At work, I had to pretend I was fine.
Pretend I had slept.
Pretend I wasn't worrying every moment about my children, their safety, their tears, their needs.
Pretend my heart wasn't cracking quietly each time I remembered that I couldn't tuck them in or hug them goodnight.

There were days when I wanted to pack my bags and go home.
Days when exhaustion sat on my shoulders like a weight I couldn't carry anymore.
Days when the loneliness became so loud that even breathing felt hard.

But every time I almost gave up, I reminded myself why I made this choice.
The sacrifices.
The visa process.
The hope I carried.
The faith that this journey would lead to something better for my family.

So I kept going.

Work demanded long hours, limited rest, and no real holidays. Salaries came late. Responsibilities piled up. There was no structure, no support system, no guidebook on how to survive emotionally while your body and spirit were running on empty.

I worked through fatigue so deep it felt like gravity.
Through headaches, tears, worry, and nights with no sleep.

Through days when I felt like I was teaching on autopilot because my mind was still back home with my family.

But I showed up.
Every day.

Even when I was breaking.
Even when I felt unseen, unsupported, and stretched beyond what any person should endure alone.

This chapter of my life was not just about working hard.
It was about working through pain, through exhaustion, through loneliness...
and still giving more than I had.

It was the beginning of a lesson I didn't know I was learning:

You can be strong for so long that people forget you are human.

Chapter 3: Carrying The Weight Alone

By the time the year was coming to an end, I was tired in ways I couldn't fully explain.
Not just physically, but emotionally — holding myself together in a country that was still teaching me how to survive one day at a time.

My contract was almost finished, and I told myself that the next job would be better.
A place with proper holidays.
A place where salaries arrived on time.
A place where I wouldn't work six days a week with no pause to breathe.
I believed I had paid my dues, and finally, something good was coming.

But instead of recognition, I received betrayal.

When I asked politely about the flight reimbursement they had promised me when I first signed the contract, everything changed.
They became distant.
Cold.
Suddenly, I was no longer an employee they valued — I was an inconvenience.

Soon after, they told me they would not renew my contract.

At first, I blamed myself.
Maybe I asked at the wrong time.
Maybe I should have waited.
Maybe I misunderstood.

But then the truth revealed itself:

They had never paid social insurance for me —
not a single month.

One whole year of work...
one whole year of showing up...
one whole year of pushing through loneliness and exhaustion...
and legally, it was as if none of it counted.

No social insurance meant no pension contributions.
No safety net.
No protection.
No medical coverage if I had needed it.
Just work — without security.

I realized that for an entire year, I had worked on trust they did not deserve.

And yet, something beautiful happened during that same time:

My husband finally joined me in China.

After months of crying alone, worrying alone, cooking alone, and waking up alone, I finally had someone beside me again.
Even though I still missed my children with every beat of my heart, having him there changed everything.

For the first time, I didn't feel like I was fighting this life alone.
If I needed to move to a new city for a better job, he would come with me.
If I was rejected, he encouraged me.
If I doubted myself, he held my hand and reminded me why I came here in the first place.

This chapter of my life was heavy, painful, and filled with lessons I never asked for.

But it was also the chapter where I learned:

Sometimes endings are not punishments.
Sometimes they are redirections — gentle or brutal — toward something better.

This was the moment I realized that I wasn't just carrying loneliness anymore...
I was carrying the courage to start again.

This chapter of my life also taught me something else I never forgot:

You can be surrounded by people at work and still feel painfully alone.
But one person who truly stands with you can give you the strength to try again.

PART II — HOPING FOR BETTER

Chapter 4: A New Workplace

After everything I had endured in my first job, stepping into a new workplace felt like stepping into light after a long tunnel.
A new city.
A new school.
A new beginning that I prayed would finally bring stability.

I arrived with lessons carved into my bones — lessons about late salaries, empty promises, and the pain of working without insurance or protection.
This time, I asked all the right questions.
Do you provide social insurance?
Do teachers get proper holidays?
Is there stability? Structure? Respect?

And for the first time, the answers seemed reassuring.
"Yes, we have insurance."
"Yes, you will have two days off every week."
"Yes, we have proper holidays — not just public holidays."
"Yes, the environment is friendly."

It felt like hope was finally breathing again.

The staff here were warm, welcoming, and far more organized. They helped me understand the schedule, the workload, and the expectations. I wasn't constantly guessing or surviving from moment to moment. There were systems in place, structure, and a sense that I could finally grow instead of just endure.

And then something even greater — something deeply emotional — lifted my spirit:

Soon, I would be going home to bring my two children to China.

The thought of my babies finally being close again made every challenge feel lighter. I missed them every day — their voices, their laughter, their small everyday stories. No one takes care of children like a mother, and no matter how brave I tried to be in my first year, a part of me remained incomplete without them.

Now there was hope that our family would be together again.
Hope that my children would wake up to my voice, not a phone screen.

Hope that I could finally work, not as a lonely parent praying across different time zones, but as a mother surrounded by the people who mattered most.

My husband was already with me, steady and supportive. And now my children would soon join us.

It felt like everything was falling into place —
a city that seemed kinder,
a workplace that felt stable,
a schedule that allowed me to breathe,
and a future that looked brighter than anything I had experienced since leaving home.

For the first time in a long time, I allowed myself to hope.
To believe that maybe this new chapter would not break me,
but rebuild me.

Chapter 5: Becoming the "Strong One"

This new workplace felt like a breath of fresh air. For the first time in a long time, life seemed to be settling into something steady, something hopeful.
The staff were friendly, the environment felt lighter, and having two days off a week felt like luxury after the year I had just survived. I finally had proper holidays — real breaks that allowed me to breathe, pause, and reconnect with myself.

I used that first long holiday to travel home.
To see my mother.
To sit with my sisters.
To be held by familiar love again.
Then came the moment that revived my entire spirit — bringing my children back with me.
Their excitement filled every corner of my heart.
And their father, my husband, stayed behind temporarily, counting down the days until we could all be together again. Knowing he was waiting, eager for his family to be reunited, made the journey feel purposeful and warm.

The kids were thrilled to start a new chapter — a new life, a new country, a new chance to be close to their mother again. Their joy gave me strength.

But even in this hopeful season, I made one mistake that many dedicated workers make:

I forgot to create boundaries.

I answered homework messages from parents late at night.
I corrected assignments on my phone after hours.
I prepared lessons long after I should have been resting.

I wanted to prove myself.
I wanted to keep my employer happy.
And because I loved teaching, it didn't feel like sacrifice — until I realized how much of my evenings were slipping away.

My home became an extension of my classroom.
My children would be talking to me while I typed out feedback.
My husband would wait for me to finish "just one more" task.

I was giving the best parts of myself to work, and whatever was left — the tired parts — to my family.

But eventually, I learned something important:

No matter how much you love your job, your family deserves the version of you that is present, not the version that is exhausted.

I began to understand that being a "strong one" didn't mean stretching myself thin.
It meant protecting my peace.
Protecting my family time.
Protecting the joy that made me a good teacher in the first place.

This chapter of my life held hope, new beginnings, and beautiful reunions.
It also held one of my greatest lessons:

Strength is not in doing everything —
it is in knowing what not to sacrifice.

For the first time in a long time, life felt like it was moving in the right direction.

I had moved to a new city where the work environment seemed warmer, the staff friendlier, and the schedule far more humane than anything I had experienced before. Two days off every week, proper holidays, and a sense of structure — it felt like relief. It felt like hope. After everything I had gone through, I finally allowed myself to breathe.

During my holiday break, I travelled home to be with my mother and sisters, to feel the warmth of family, and to gather the strength I had lost without even realizing it. And the best part — I brought my children back with me. They were excited, full of questions and curiosity, ready to start a new chapter. And my husband, who had stayed behind so I could travel freely, could hardly wait for us to return. We were finally going to be together again under one roof, and that alone made everything feel worth it.

But with this fresh beginning came a mistake I didn't see coming.

I gave too much.

I blurred the line between work and home without even noticing. After hours, while I should have been resting or bonding with my family, I found myself still answering homework questions, correcting exercises, responding to parents, and preparing lessons late into the night. I wanted to show my new workplace that I was dependable, dedicated, and professional. I wanted to be the teacher they could trust with anything.

And I loved my job — truly. Teaching filled my days with joy and purpose, and the children brought out the best in me. But loving your work does not mean giving it all of you. I learned this lesson too late.

In my effort to be the "strong one," the reliable one, the always-available one, I slowly began to disappear from the spaces that mattered most. Once again, I was putting myself last — not because anyone asked me to, but because I didn't know how to set boundaries. I didn't know how to say, "This can wait until tomorrow."

That is how I became the one everyone could count on...

Even when I was tired.
Even when I needed rest.
Even when I needed to be a mother and a wife
before anything else.

I carried everything — work, home, emotion,
responsibility — because I wanted to keep the
peace, keep the harmony, keep the approval.

I didn't know yet that this kind of strength comes
with a cost.

A cost my body would soon make me pay.

PART III — WHEN THE BODY BEGS FOR REST

CHAPTER 6 — WHEN MY BODY STARTED WARNING ME

No one warned me that "40 working hours"
before summer holidays could mean a marathon.
A slow, silent drain of energy.
A workload that stretched beyond what the body
could reasonably carry.
I thought I was doing what every good teacher
does — pushing through, showing up, giving more
than I had.
But long before the collapse happened, my body
had already begun whispering its warnings.

At first, it was small things:
the constant tiredness, the heaviness in my legs,
the dizziness when I stood up too fast.
Then the whispers became louder.
I was sleeping only 3–4 hours a night, barely
eating because exhaustion took away my
appetite.
Each day, I poured everything I had into the
students, and each night, I came home with
nothing left for myself.

I didn't know that anaemia works quietly —
that low haemoglobin slowly starves your organs
of oxygen,
that your brain begins to misinterpret signals,
that sleep deprivation, stress, and poor nutrition
only make the condition worse.

But my body knew.

And one night, while preparing a PPT for a lesson,
the breaking point came.
I was choosing cartoon images — cute, colorful,
harmless —
when suddenly they didn't look harmless
anymore.
Their faces twisted in a way that terrified me.
My skin crawled.
A wave of itchiness rushed over me.
Every picture looked wrong.
Every color felt too loud.

I closed the laptop, convinced I was just tired.

But the next morning, inside the classroom, it
happened again.

The moment I opened the PPT, the same images triggered a panic so strong I ran out of the classroom and locked myself inside the bathroom.
I cried because I didn't understand what was happening.
Cartoons — something I had loved all my life — suddenly looked monstrous.

My colleagues witnessed the episode and urged me to go to the hospital.
But when I arrived, no one spoke English.
Trying to explain my symptoms with gestures and translation apps was nearly impossible.
They asked if I had a family history of mental illness.
I shook my head.
I was confused, scared, and alone — being told something was wrong with my mind when, inside, something told me this wasn't the whole truth.

My husband refused to accept their conclusion.
He could see the exhaustion.
He knew I hadn't been sleeping or eating properly.
He insisted we travel to a bigger city with better resources, and that decision may have saved me.

There, we met a doctor who spoke fluent English. For the first time, I could explain everything clearly — the fear, the visual distortions, the insomnia, the breathlessness, the weakness, the itching, the mental fog.

He ordered a full set of tests:
blood work
CT scan
MRI
neurological evaluation

And the answer appeared in the blood test like a loud alarm my body had been ringing for months:

My haemoglobin was dangerously low.
Critically low.
Low enough to cause hallucination-like visual distortions.
Low enough to mimic mental health symptoms.
Low enough to make my body feel like it was shutting down.

The doctor explained it simply:
"When the brain doesn't receive enough oxygen, it misfires.
Stress multiplies the effect.
Sleep deprivation multiplies it again.

Your body has been carrying more than it can handle."

Suddenly everything made sense.

The weakness.
The emotional breakdowns.
The racing thoughts.
The blurry vision.
The fear that came out of nowhere.
The exhaustion so deep I forgot to eat.

It wasn't madness.
It was anaemia — severe, untreated anaemia —
worsened by overwork and months of ignoring
my body's cries for rest.

I was given iron supplements, vitamins, and a
strict warning:
reduce screen time, sleep more, eat regularly,
rest, or your body will collapse again.

So I listened for once.
I slowed down.
On my off days, instead of preparing lessons, I
stepped outside.
I watched trees.
I breathed fresh air.

I allowed myself to disconnect from work —
something I should have done long before.

This chapter became a lesson I never wanted but
desperately needed:
the body doesn't break suddenly —
it whispers, warns, begs...
until it finally screams.

And mine screamed because I kept trying to be
superhuman in a job that demanded more than
my health could give.

CHAPTER 7 — The Pregnancy I Hoped For

Healing from anaemia was not a quick journey, but day by day, my body slowly found its way back to me.

For weeks, even looking at a cartoon character felt terrifying — the strange visual distortions, the itchy skin, the crawling sensation under my flesh. But slowly, the fear began to fade. My skin stopped reacting. My heartbeat steadied. My sleep returned in small, precious pieces. And one morning, I opened a cartoon PPT for class and nothing happened. No fear. No crawling sensations. No breakdown.
Just relief.

Returning to work after that storm felt like stepping back into sunlight. I wasn't fully myself yet, but I was functioning — teaching, laughing again, breathing again. The financial strain of all the medical bills was heavy, but thank God for my husband. He stepped in without hesitation, using money from his business and online work to cover everything that needed to be paid.

That season taught me something I never truly understood before:
You don't fully grasp the meaning of "in sickness and in health" until sickness sits inside your home.

For almost a month, my husband carried all of us — cooking every day, searching online for the best foods to rebuild my iron levels, taking care of the kids, watching me closely for any sign of relapse. He made soups, vegetables, meat, iron-rich meals... and I gained weight because for the first time in a long time, someone was feeding me with love and intention.

Slowly, life felt like life again.

And then, just when I thought the worst was behind me, something unexpected happened.

I found out I was pregnant.

A baby was not part of our plans — not now, not in the middle of recovering, not in a foreign country with so much instability around me. But life does not always ask for our permission. And falling pregnant while on contraceptives was the last thing I ever imagined.

Still... when the second line appeared on the test, I felt shock first... then disbelief... and then something gentle.

I didn't believe in abortion, and despite the timing, despite the chaos, despite the fear — this was a life. A heartbeat waiting to grow. My husband was overjoyed the moment I told him. His whole face lit up. And in that moment, I knew we were choosing this baby together.

We accepted the pregnancy with hope.
We talked about names.
We imagined a tiny person joining our family.
After surviving so much, maybe this was our new beginning.

I didn't know then that this joy would be short-lived.
I didn't know that everything was about to break again.

But for a brief moment, we were happy — truly, deeply happy — and that happiness deserves its place in the story.

PART IV — THE BREAKING POINT

CHAPTER 8 — The Day Everything Went Silent

I was still healing from anaemia when life surprised me with something I didn't expect — a positive pregnancy test.
It wasn't planned, yet somehow it felt like a blessing.
A new beginning.
A soft promise after months of struggle.

My husband was over the moon.
I was still catching up emotionally, but I accepted it with the same love that had carried me through every hardship.
We even started whispering baby names at night.
It felt like life was finally giving back what it had taken.

But the first doctor's visit didn't give us the reassurance we hoped for.

They saw a dark sac on the screen — a gestational sac — but nothing inside it.
No baby shape.
No yolk sac.
No heartbeat.
Just silence.

The doctor said it might simply be too early, that maybe the embryo was "still small," that we should wait.
So we waited.
And every day of waiting felt like a year.

I began injections — one painful shot every day for two full weeks — meant to support the pregnancy, strengthen the hormones, give the baby every possible chance.
Each injection left a sting, but I endured it with hope.
Hope that the next scan would show our miracle.

But the next ultrasound looked just like the first.
The sac grew, but remained empty.
A dark circle where life was supposed to be.

The doctor ordered another follow-up the next week.
Then another.
Each time we held our breath.
Each time the room stayed quiet.

People talk about hearing a baby's heartbeat as a moment of joy.
No one prepares you for the moment when you don't hear one.
No one prepares you for the silence — the kind that squeezes your chest, the kind that steals your breath before the doctor even says the words.

Still, the doctors didn't want to rush.
Sometimes pregnancies are slower to develop.
Sometimes dates can be off.
Sometimes miracles happen late.

So I stepped into the clinic week after week, letting gel hit my stomach, watching the same dark image appear on the screen.
Hope rising, hope falling.
Hope rising again.

Until the day the doctor finally stopped searching.

Her face told me the truth before her words did.

"The sac is growing," she said softly, "but the embryo is not. This is an anembryonic pregnancy."

A pregnancy without a developing baby.
A life that never formed.
A dream that never had the chance to breathe.

I stared at the screen — that familiar dark circle — and felt myself sink into a kind of grief I didn't know how to name.
I wasn't just losing a pregnancy.
I was losing everything I had held onto through the injections, the appointments, the prayers, the waiting.

I walked out of the hospital with instructions.
I needed a procedure — a uterine evacuation — to remove what my body could not release on its own.

It didn't matter how strong I thought I was.
It didn't matter that this baby wasn't planned.
It didn't matter that I had tried to prepare myself.

Nothing prepares you for the moment hope collapses inside your own body.

Nothing prepares you for the silence.

CHAPTER 9 — SURGERY AND INVISIBLE PAIN

They say grief has many forms, but nothing prepares you for the kind that begins in a hospital room—sterile, bright, and too quiet for what your heart is screaming inside.

When the doctor told me the pregnancy could not continue, my body felt numb, but my mind stayed awake in the worst way. I tried to stay strong. I tried to breathe through it. But strength has limits, and mine finally reached its edge the moment they wheeled me into the operating room.

The lights above me were cold.
The room smelled of disinfectant.
Metal instruments clinked softly in the background.

And that was the moment it became real.

I started to cry.

Not the silent kind.
Not the kind you wipe away quickly so no one notices.

These tears came from somewhere deep inside—a place you don't know exists until it breaks.

My doctor, who didn't speak a word of English, saw my tears before I could hide them. She paused, gently placed her hand in mine, and held it tightly. She couldn't say the words I needed to hear, but she didn't have to. The softness in her eyes said enough.

She wiped my tears with a small tissue she pulled from the tray, her hand shaking slightly—as if she wished she could take the pain from me but didn't know how. We had always communicated through a translation app, but in that moment, language didn't matter. Humanity did.

Just before the anesthesia pulled me under, I looked toward the door—hoping to catch one last glimpse of my husband. He wasn't allowed inside, but he waited right outside, holding everything together for both of us.

I could still picture his face—
the sadness he tried to hide,
the fear sitting behind his eyes,
the strength he forced himself to show because
he knew I needed it.

And when it was over—when the room stopped
spinning and my eyes finally opened—he was the
first person I saw.

No words.
No explanations.
No questions.

Just his hand reaching for mine, steady and
warm.

We walked out of the hospital together in silence
—hand in hand, side by side. A silence that wasn't
empty, but full. Full of the things we could not yet
say. Full of the pain we didn't know how to name.

Outside, he finally spoke.

"Everything will be okay," he said softly.
"It's not your fault."

And I believed him—not because the pain had disappeared, but because he had always been my strength. Even in that moment, when both our hearts were breaking, he carried mine as gently as he could.

That day, I learned something new about grief.
It doesn't always look like screaming or collapsing.
Sometimes it looks like walking quietly beside the person you love, both of you hurting, both of you holding hope with whatever pieces you have left.

That day changed me.
It changed us.
And it became a chapter of my life I never expected to write.

CHAPTER 10 · Messages That Came Too Soon

Rest was the one thing my body desperately needed after the surgery.
The doctor had gently explained that my body had been through trauma — internal, invisible, but very real — and she recommended that I take two weeks to recover. She wrote the rest note herself, stamped and official, as if giving me permission to stop being strong for once.

And I handed that note to my employer, trusting that compassion would follow.

But compassion did not come.

Instead, what came were messages.

Not the kind that ask how you're healing.
Not the kind that say "take your time."
Not the kind that acknowledge loss.

They were messages asking me when I could come back to work.

I was still in pain — the deep, quiet, aching pain of a body trying to piece itself together again — when my phone buzzed. At first, I thought it might be a friend checking on me, or my family sending love from home.

But it wasn't.

It was work asking whether I could return sooner than expected.

The words on the screen felt heavier than they looked.
I remember staring at the message, still lying in bed, still bleeding, still sore from the inside, wondering how anyone could imagine that four days was enough to recover from losing a pregnancy — physically or emotionally.

I wasn't just healing from a procedure.
I was healing from a loss.
A loss I didn't choose. A loss I didn't want.
A loss that had already taken too much from me.

And yet, somehow, the world around me seemed impatient for me to hurry up and move on.

No one from work asked how I was feeling.
No one asked if the pain had lessened.
No one acknowledged the surgery, the grief, or
the silence that follows this kind of heartbreak.

What I received were reminders of schedules.
Reminders of duties.
Reminders that the workplace was waiting — even
when I wasn't ready to stand.

It made me realize something painful but true:

Some workplaces don't see the human being
behind the employee.
They only see the work.

And when you can't give them what they want,
they notice your absence more than they value
your presence.

I lay there reading their messages, my body still
fragile, my emotions still raw, and I wondered how
quickly people forget that healing is not just
physical.
It is emotional.
Mental.
Spiritual.

And you cannot rush any of those.

Their messages didn't just come too soon —
they came at a time when I needed
understanding, not pressure.
When I needed space, not reminders.
When I needed kindness, not expectations.

In that moment, I learned another truth about
working far from home:

Sometimes, when tragedy strikes, the silence
from your workplace hurts almost as much as the
loss itself.

Because that silence says:
"We see your role.
We see your value.
But we do not see you."

And that realization stays with you long after the
messages stop.

CHAPTER 11: The Insurance That Was Not Insurance

For a long time, I believed I was protected.

When I accepted the job, I had asked about insurance — because after everything I had experienced in my first year abroad, I had learned how important it was.
And I was told, confidently and without hesitation:

"Yes, we have insurance."

I took that as security.
I took it as the reassurance I needed.
I took it as a promise.

It wasn't until my miscarriage — until the moment I needed support the most — that I learned the truth.

There was no medical insurance.
No maternity insurance.
No social insurance of any kind.

What I had been given was not the legal insurance employees are supposed to have — but a commercial accident plan, something that looked official on the surface but meant almost nothing when reality hit.

At first, I couldn't understand why the hospital bills were piling up and the school wasn't stepping in to help. I assumed it was an error, a misunderstanding, something that could be fixed with one conversation.

But instead of clarity, I was met with hesitation.
With uncertainty.
With shifting explanations.

Only then did I begin to piece together the truth: The "insurance" they provided me did not cover pregnancy, miscarriage, surgery, or even basic medical care. It wasn't meant to. It was never meant to protect me the way true employee insurance should.

And what hurt the most wasn't the money — it was the realization that I had been carrying a false sense of security all along.

When I needed medical support, there was none.
When I was physically weak, I had to find strength alone.
When I was emotionally shattered, I also had to carry financial stress on my shoulders.

It felt like betrayal, but not the loud, dramatic kind.
It was the quiet kind — the kind that sinks in slowly, hour by hour, bill after bill, until you finally admit to yourself:

"I was never protected."

And in that realization came a much deeper question:

If I, a foreign teacher who showed up every day, who gave everything, who smiled through exhaustion —
was never truly covered,
never truly supported,
never truly valued...

Then what did my work really mean to the people I trusted?

This chapter of my life taught me something I never expected to learn abroad:

Sometimes you can give your whole heart to a place...
and only then discover it was running on promises, not protection.

It wasn't just about insurance.
It was about what it symbolized —
the difference between being employed and being looked after,
between being contracted and being human,
between being useful and being valued.

And it was in the middle of my healing —
physically, emotionally, spiritually — that I had to face one painful truth:

I had been working without a safety net in a place where I believed I had one.

But this realization didn't break me.
It opened my eyes.
It taught me what to never accept again.
It taught me what protection truly means.
It prepared me for every chapter that followed.

CHAPTER 12 — When Support Depends on Your Passport

I used to believe that workplaces were built on fairness — that dedication, effort, and professionalism were the foundations of how you were treated.

But slowly, quietly, I learned something else.

In some environments, the difference between being protected and being left alone has nothing to do with how hard you work...

It has everything to do with whether you are local or foreign.

This realization didn't hit me all at once.
It arrived in small experiences that I tried to ignore until they could no longer be unseen.

It arrived the day I discovered that the local teachers had full coverage —
pension contributions, medical insurance, support during pregnancy or miscarriage —
while foreign teachers worked without any of it.

It arrived when I learned that locals contributed a portion toward social insurance and the school paid the rest —
but foreigners were not enrolled at all.

It arrived the day I found out that if a local teacher gave birth or suffered a miscarriage, they were protected —
but when I went through the same pain, I wasn't.

It arrived when a colleague from the country — seeing how overwhelmed I was with medical bills — offered to help me ask for a salary advance.
She got it immediately.

Yet when I asked, I was told it wasn't possible.

Later, she quietly handed me the money, explaining that she had pretended the request was for herself.
I borrowed it from her and paid her back, but the truth stung:

It wasn't the loan that hurt.
It was the realization that foreign teachers like me were not seen or supported the same way.

And perhaps the most painful part was knowing this wasn't about performance.

Foreign teachers taught long hours —
often double the duration of the classes taught by locals —
poured energy into lessons, represented the school proudly, and gave everything to the students...

Yet when it came to protection, security, or basic benefits,
we stood alone.

Not because we didn't try.
Not because we weren't loyal.
Not because we weren't capable.

But because we were foreign.

This chapter of my life taught me something deep and uncomfortable:

Discrimination isn't always loud.
Sometimes it is polite.
Sometimes it is hidden behind "policy."
Sometimes it is wrapped in excuses about contracts, rules, or paperwork.

But no matter how quietly it hides,
its impact is the same.

It leaves you feeling invisible where you work the
hardest.
It leaves you unprotected where you give the
most.
It leaves you wondering why humanity has
borders in places where compassion should not.

All I ever wanted was fairness —
not special treatment,
not privilege,
just the same protection any worker deserves.

Because foreign or not,
we feel, we bleed, we grieve, we break —
and we deserve to be treated as human beings.

PART VI — RISING AGAIN

CHAPTER 13 — The Day I Stopped Pretending to Be Okay

There comes a moment in every person's life when silence becomes too heavy to carry.

For months, I had held myself together with thin threads of strength — the kind that look strong from the outside but fray quietly from within. I taught classes with a smile. I greeted colleagues with warmth. I laughed when people expected me to laugh.
And every night, when the world stopped watching, I unraveled.

But grief has a way of finding the cracks. It seeps through them, gently at first, then all at once.

The day I stopped pretending happened quietly. No dramatic moment. No breakdown in public. No confrontation.
Just a simple morning when my body refused to keep holding everything inside.

I woke up, sat at the edge of the bed, and felt something shift.
Not physically — emotionally.

Like a truth finally pushing through the weight of everything I had been trying to hide.

I wasn't okay.
And for the first time, I allowed myself to say it.

I had survived loneliness, overwork, exhaustion, anaemia, medical bills, fear, and heartbreak.
I had survived a miscarriage I never saw coming.
I had survived the unexpected surgery, the grief afterward, and the emotional emptiness that followed.

But what I could no longer survive was pretending.

Pretending I wasn't hurting.
Pretending I wasn't tired.
Pretending I wasn't grieving something that had been small but deeply loved.
Pretending I wasn't overwhelmed by the pressure to be strong in a place where strength had become my only identity.

That morning, I stopped hiding my tears from myself.
I let them flow — not quietly, not controlled — but honestly.

Tears for my body.
Tears for the baby I carried briefly.
Tears for the woman I had forced myself to be
when I was hurting the most.

And something remarkable happened.

The world didn't fall apart when I admitted I
wasn't okay.
I didn't become weaker.
I didn't lose anything.
If anything, I gained something I had been missing
for far too long:

permission to be human.

I realized that healing doesn't begin when the
wound closes — it begins when you acknowledge
that you're wounded.

That day, I stopped performing strength and
started choosing honesty.
I stopped carrying everything alone and let
myself lean on the people who truly cared — my
husband, my children, and the version of myself
who had survived too much to break now.

The day I stopped pretending was not the end of my suffering.
But it was the beginning of my healing.

It was the day I learned that strength isn't the absence of pain —
it's the courage to face it.

It was the day I chose myself.

And that choice changed everything that came after.

CHAPTER 14 — When Teachers Bleed

(A Poem)

🌿 When Teachers Bleed

I am the one who smiles for children,
even on days my own heart trembles.
I am the hands that clap,
the voice that sings,
the warmth that makes a room feel safe.

But today —
my body is healing from a storm
no parent would wish on themselves.
An empty cradle shaped itself inside me,
and my womb and spirit
are still learning how to breathe again.

You came into my home
with shoes clean,
but hearts untouched.

You looked at my face
as if strength means the absence of pain,
as if a woman must stand
the moment she falls.

But the wound is inside.
It doesn't limp,
doesn't bruise,
doesn't bleed where eyes can see.
It bleeds where memories sleep,
where hope once whispered a name.

Teaching is joy.
Teaching is giving.
Teaching is smiling with your whole soul.
And my soul —
my soul is still gathering itself
from the pieces I lost that night.

I am not refusing.
I am recovering.
I am not weak.
I am wounded.

And wounds — real wounds —
need time.

So let me heal
before I hold a classroom again.
Let me breathe
before I must brighten the world again.
Let me be human
before I must be "Teacher" again.

Because even teachers bleed.
Even teachers lose.
Even teachers break.

And when I return —
I will rise whole.
I will rise softer.
I will rise stronger.

But today,
I just need to be allowed
to be a woman
who loved,
who lost,
and who deserves
to heal.

CHAPTER 15 — WHAT EMPLOYERS NEVER THINK ABOUT

Workplaces often see the surface of a person — the punctuality, the productivity, the energy, the smile. They see the lesson plans, the tasks completed, the deadlines met. They measure attendance, performance, and output.

But what they rarely see is the human behind all of that.

They don't see the nights a worker barely sleeps because their mind is fighting battles no job description could ever prepare for.
They don't see the moments before work when someone wipes away tears, so children, students, or colleagues won't ask questions they don't have the strength to answer.
They don't see the meals skipped because exhaustion has replaced appetite.
They don't see the courage it takes to show up after heartbreak, after loss, after illness, after life has ripped through someone's world.

Employers forget that the people they rely on —
the ones who keep classrooms alive, offices
running, and businesses functioning — are human
beings first.
Not machines.
Not numbers.
Not replaceable labor.

Human beings with bodies that reach limits.
Human beings with hearts that break.
Human beings with families who need them and
children who look for them at the end of each
day.

Support is not only about policies, insurance, or
regulations — although those matter deeply.
Support is also about empathy, timing, and
understanding.
It is about recognizing that a person cannot pour
out joy when they are still learning to breathe
through their pain.
It is about understanding that healing is not
laziness, and rest is not abandonment.

Compassion costs nothing, yet changes
everything.

A workplace becomes safer the moment it remembers that employees are not tools — they are people.
A workplace becomes healthier the moment it stops asking, "When will you return?" and instead asks, "How are you feeling, and how can we support you?"
A workplace becomes stronger the moment it realizes that loyalty grows in environments where dignity is protected, and vulnerability is not punished.

Because here is the truth:

No employer loses anything by caring.
But they lose everything when they forget that the people who work for them carry lives, bodies, and emotions that continue long after the shift ends.

And perhaps the greatest lesson is this:

When an employer stands by a worker during their hardest moments, that support becomes a story — a powerful one — that lasts far beyond the job itself.

But when an employer turns away during someone's suffering, that too becomes a story.

And those stories matter.

They shape futures.
They shape decisions.
They shape who stays... and who walks away.

This chapter is not about blame — it is about awareness.
It is a reminder that behind every teacher, every staff member, every employee, there is a whole human life unfolding.

And all it takes to honor that life is kindness, fairness, and the understanding that work should never come at the cost of a person's health or humanity.

CHAPTER 16 — CHOOSING MYSELF AGAIN

There comes a moment in every person's life when survival quietly turns into awakening.
A moment when you stop asking, "Why is this happening to me?"
And begin to ask, "Why am I still allowing it?"

For me, that moment arrived slowly, like light sliding under a closed door.

After everything I had been through — the exhaustion, the anaemia, the loneliness, the pregnancy, the loss, the medical bills, the legal questions, the unequal treatment — I realized something I had forgotten while carrying everyone else:

I still had myself.

The woman who left home with hope.
The woman who survived a year alone.
The woman who built a life from scratch in a place where she didn't even speak the language.
The woman who worked through exhaustion, who loved her students, who tried her best even when her body was giving up.

The woman who held her family together from thousands of kilometers away.
The woman who lost a child... yet continued breathing, step by step.

I was still her.

And she deserved compassion too.

I had spent so long being strong that I didn't realise strength also means knowing when to walk away.
When to stop allowing workplaces to decide your worth.
When to stop proving yourself to people who only see the surface and not the heart.
When to stop giving loyalty to environments that cannot give humanity in return.

Choosing myself was not a dramatic moment.
It was a quiet decision, whispered in my spirit:

"I choose my health.
I choose my peace.
I choose my future."

I realized that healing is not just about resting your body — it's also about releasing the places that hurt your mind and weighed down your soul.

Healing meant understanding that I was more than the exhaustion, more than the grief, more than the unfair treatment.

Healing meant seeing my worth clearly again.

It meant remembering that:

- I was a mother before I was an employee.
- I was a woman before I was a teacher.
- I was a human being before anyone tried to define me by my job.

And no job, no contract, no title could ever be more important than my life or my well-being.

This chapter of my story wasn't just about leaving a workplace.
It was about leaving behind a version of myself that tolerated pain quietly.
It was about closing a door that drained me, so I could open one that restored me.

Choosing myself didn't make me selfish.
It made me free.

And as I stepped forward — with my husband by
my side, with my children waiting to be held, with
my body slowly healing — I understood
something powerful:

Sometimes you don't get the ending you hoped
for.
But you still get the chance to begin again.

And beginning again, on your own terms...
is its own kind of victory.

PART VII — THE LESSONS WE CARRY

Chapter 17: What Employers Should Do

Workplaces are built on people — not policies, not buildings, not reputations.
Real people with bodies that get tired, families they miss, emotions they hide, and lives they carry quietly behind their smiles.

Every employer who understands this will always have happier staff, lower turnover, and a stronger, more loyal team.

Here are the principles that turn workplaces into communities — principles every employer should embrace:

1. Provide Equal Protection for Every Employee

Insurance, benefits, and safety nets should never depend on nationality, contract type, or origin.
Every worker deserves:
- medical protection
- emergency coverage
- maternity and sickness support
- workplace safety
- fair treatment

When employees feel secure, they perform better — because fear is no longer part of their job.

2. Respect Sick Leave and Mental Health

A body that is healing cannot give you its best.
A mind that is breaking cannot perform with clarity.
When employees are ill, recovering from trauma, or grieving, the most powerful thing an employer can offer is compassion — and time.

Always have substitute staff ready.
No one should feel guilty for being human.

3. Celebrate Your Employees' Humanity

A simple "You're doing a great job" goes further than you think.
A birthday message, a small celebration, or acknowledging effort builds a workplace where employees feel seen, not used.

When people feel valued, they stay.
They carry the company in their heart, not just on their schedule.

4. Avoid Comparison — Embrace Encouragement

No two employees are the same.
Never compare one staff member to another.
Instead:

- celebrate strengths
- guide gently
- correct respectfully
- encourage consistently

People thrive where they are uplifted, not measured.

5. Provide Support Systems, Especially for Foreign Workers

Employees far from home carry invisible weight — loneliness, cultural shock, language barriers, and emotional strain.
Offer them:

- counselling or someone to talk to
- regular check-ins
- help navigating the system
- understanding when family issues arise

Support doesn't weaken workers — it strengthens the bond between employer and employee.

6. Maintain Clear Communication and Honesty

Keep your promises.
Clarify expectations.
Be transparent about policies.
When employees know they can trust your word, the workplace becomes stable, predictable, and fair.

Trust is the currency of leadership.

7. Protect Breaks, Days Off, and Rest

Rest is not laziness.
Rest is necessary.
When employees finish work, let them disconnect fully.
Encourage healthy boundaries.

An employee who rests returns with energy, creativity, and love for their job.

8. Always Have Enough Staff

One person should not carry the weight of an entire team.
Plan ahead, hire enough teachers/workers, and keep substitutes available.

Preparedness prevents burnout — for everyone.

9. Offer Growth, Not Just Work

Train employees.
Help them improve.
Guide them professionally.
People stay longer where they feel like they are growing, not just surviving.

10. Remember: Employees Are People First
They have families.
They have emotions.
They have bodies that get tired and hearts that break.

When employers treat workers with humanity, loyalty grows naturally.
And when people feel safe, respected, and valued — they give the best of themselves willingly.

A great workplace is not one where employees are perfect.
It's one where employees feel protected, appreciated, and understood.

Human first.
Employee second.
Always.

CHAPTER 17 — WHAT EMPLOYEES MUST ALSO PRACTICE

Workplaces thrive when both sides honour their responsibilities.
Just as employers carry the duty to protect, support, and respect their staff, employees also carry responsibilities that shape the environment they work in.

This is not about perfection.
It is about professionalism — the silent agreement that makes a workplace humane and functional.

Here is what employees, including people like me, must remember:

1. Show up with integrity

Be honest about your work, your abilities, and your limits.
Integrity builds trust — the foundation of every healthy workplace.

2. Communicate openly and respectfully

Ask questions when something is unclear.
Express concerns before they become problems.
And do your best to communicate with patience, even when the situation is stressful.

3. Honour your working hours

Give your best during the hours you are paid for.
Stay focused.
Be present.
Your time and your employer's time deserve
mutual respect.

4. Maintain professionalism — even when you're hurting

We all come into work carrying private battles.
But professionalism means not letting those
battles spill into our responsibilities.
This doesn't mean pretending to be okay — it
means doing your best to balance humanity with
duty.

5. Take care of your health

Burnout helps no one — not you, not your
students, not your colleagues.
Listen to your body.
Seek help early.
Rest when it is necessary.
A healthy employee is a stronger employee.

6. Respect company policies — and speak up when they are unclear

Following rules is part of professionalism.
But responsible employees also ask questions
when policies seem inconsistent or need
improvement.

7. Strive for growth

Learn.
Improve.
Adapt.
Bring new ideas to the table.
A workplace grows when its people grow.

8. Build a positive environment

Kindness, collaboration, and empathy go a long
way.
You never know what your coworkers are facing
outside of work.
Be someone who brings calm, not chaos.

9. Separate work time from personal time appropriately

Dedication is admirable — but sacrificing all your personal hours eventually harms you and your family.
Healthy boundaries do not make you a bad employee.
They make you a balanced one.

10. Support your colleagues

Share knowledge.
Cover for each other when necessary.
Speak up if someone is mistreated.
Workplaces improve when employees stand together.

11. Stay accountable

When mistakes happen (and they always do),
acknowledge them with maturity.
Accountability earns respect — excuses don't.

12. Remember that professionalism does not mean silence

Being a "good employee" does not mean
tolerating mistreatment.
It means handling situations with dignity:

- asking questions,
- raising concerns,
- and advocating for yourself respectfully and confidently.

A healthy workplace is a partnership.
Employers and employees both contribute to the
environment, the culture, and the success of the
organization.

This chapter is not about blaming employees — it
is about reminding us that we also have power in
shaping the spaces where we work.

Professionalism, kindness, and responsibility
build trust.
And trust builds the workplaces we all deserve.

CLOSING CHAPTER — "The Lesson I Carry Forward"

There comes a moment in every journey when you stop looking backward with pain and begin looking forward with clarity.
For me, that moment arrived quietly — not in a hospital, not in a meeting, not during the hardest days, but in the silence afterward, when the dust finally settled and I was left alone with my truth.

I came to this country with hope.
I stayed with determination.
I survived with strength I didn't know I had.

But I am leaving with something far greater:

wisdom.

Wisdom about work.
Wisdom about people.
Wisdom about the human heart and how far it can stretch before it breaks.
Wisdom about boundaries, dignity, and the courage it takes to stand up for yourself when you feel small.

This experience taught me that even the strongest among us can be tired.
Even the most dedicated employees can be mistreated.
Even the most loving teachers can carry wounds that students will never see.

But it also taught me something else — something beautiful:

We rise.

Not because life becomes easy.
Not because people suddenly become kinder.
But because we choose to rise.
Because something inside us refuses to stay broken.
Because the human spirit is built to rebuild.

I survived the loneliness of starting over.
I survived the exhaustion of giving more than my body had left.
I survived illness, grief, and difficult conversations that shook me to my core.
I survived days when I felt invisible... and nights when I felt too seen.

But I also survived because I was not alone.

My husband stood beside me.
My children kept me going.
My faith, my resilience, and my sense of purpose
pulled me out from places I didn't think I would
escape.

And today, as I close this chapter of my life, I do
not close it with bitterness.
I close it with understanding.

Understanding that not every environment
deserves your loyalty.
Understanding that silence is not strength.
Understanding that rest is not weakness.
Understanding that you are allowed to walk away
from places that do not protect you.
Understanding that your health — physical,
mental, emotional — is not something you
negotiate.

This story is not just about what broke me.
It is also about what rebuilt me.

It is a reminder that behind every employee is a
human being.
A story.
A heartbeat.
A home full of people who love them.

A life that exists long after working hours are over.

If there is one message I want to leave with anyone reading this — whether teacher, employer, or someone simply navigating life — let it be this:

Be human first.
Everything else comes second.

Because when workplaces forget the human, they lose the very soul of what makes work meaningful.
But when they honour it — when they see, protect, and value their people — they build something stronger than any contract: trust, loyalty, and genuine dedication.

My journey has not been easy.
It has not been gentle.
But it has shaped me into someone more aware, more grounded, and more compassionate.

And now, I step into the next chapter of my life carrying this truth:

I am not the same woman who boarded that plane.
I am stronger.

I am wiser.
I am healed — or at least healing.
And I am choosing myself, my family, and my future with a courage I did not have before.

This is not the end.
It is the beginning of a new, better, brighter chapter — one I am writing with my own hands, in my own strength, and on my own terms.

Here's to healing.
Here's to growth.
Here's to becoming whole again.

And here's to every worker who has ever bled silently:

May your story remind you that you deserve care, dignity, and respect — not just as an employee, but as a human being.

About The Author

Thuli Marutle Leigh is a South African–born international ESL teacher and storyteller whose work is rooted in compassion, resilience, and the lived experiences of women and foreign workers around the world. Her years abroad — navigating unfamiliar cultures, raising a family, and rebuilding herself after personal and professional hardship — shaped her voice into one that speaks honestly about courage, dignity, and the human heart.

She is the author of more than 30 books, spanning children's stories, educational phonics, personal empowerment, and social awareness. Through her writing, Thuli gives language to the silent struggles many people carry, reminding readers that strength is not the absence of pain, but the courage to rise after it. Her work continues to inspire both young learners and adults, offering hope, understanding, and a reminder that every human story deserves to be heard.

www.ingramcontent.com/pod-product-compliance
Lightning Source LLC
Chambersburg PA
CBHW031447280326
41927CB00037B/378